EARLY HARVEST

POEMS NEW AND SELECTED

BY
EUPHRATES ARNAUT MOSS

UNBOUND
CONTENT

Englewood NJ
2014

ISBN 978-1-936373-30-7

Published in the United States by Unbound Content,
LLC, Englewood, NJ.
Author photo: ©2014, by Jenny Moreno.
The poems in this collection are all original and
previously unpublished with the exception of those
credited otherwise.

EARLY HARVEST
Poems New and Selected
First edition 2014

UNBOUND
CONTENT

Sometimes you can see much better—
When observing things obscure,
To look upon them indirectly ...
Than to watch them all the more.

—2008

Table of Contents

PART I — From Pomes Fivedoloursadozen (2010)

PART II — Excess

PART I — From Pomes Fivedoloursadozen (2010)

Moth

"Here I sit and sup upon the finest of words
And yet my heart stands barren,
Empty as a drunkard's flask long after last call."

Could you ever feel like the Artist
Working endlessly at his Cantos?
Then trying John Adams, Odysseus, and Pisan.
Still working, beleaguered and now listless as a sloth
What would you do
After you ate a Gold Bug?
Would you flail at the door?
Striking fancies running
        running madly 'Cross your floor

And yet you flit around and sit
As the new fog nips the slits
New fog still the same old sight
Sitting down in the dark of night
New fog, old fog's paramour

But I am happy
Now but still the more
"I am happy,
And that is all you need to know."
How could you fail with Dolphy at your side?
Your past employer slinks
And is cribbing all the sweets
The murmur of retreats

EUPHRATES ARNAUT MOSS

As the swarming figurine stands fast outside the door
A smiling gentle ward, creeping through

Finding one so humble as to sit and talk awhile
I forgot just what it's like to purse my lips and smile

As a moth near your open flame
My wings lit afire unfocused
A stroke of the sane
"You don't have to open fire like this!"
Open fire in the morning's moistening mist
I fall to the floor sere after the tryst
I chew on a scone and Thin out my lips
Endless rocking cradle "Death" in tiny slips

My wings now singed, now black
As I plummet towards the floor
None within I more adore

How could I swim through the air
And let the fire consume my wings?
Spastic shudders and endless groans
As a nasty Shelob makes its way
'Twas foolhardy to let the fire
        Consume my wings

The Shelob slips across the blade in a zimmer frame
Manacled and lacking its much-needed milk
She snorted in the seaven sleepers den

EARLY HARVEST

Shot the human race with a mighty gun
Dry like an August noon-day sunbath

And I, your protege, have swayed delayed dismayed
Clichéd and rolled in round the pound for pound
Swinging softly hearing sound
Speaking madly over time upon the mound
Only to resound upon a bitter ground-out noun
Close mine eyes to dream — lay down
And STILL I cannot help but frown
As though the words that would've found
A way to get my mind around
That little clowning thing in town
— But I flew to close

My wings, now my soul?
My soul it was there
When I flew so freely
My soul! My soul!
I am now amongst the embers
The dying embers now, my heart
My heart lying amongst to be set free
Set free the new Disappearer
Disappear the spirited away

Finding one so humble as to sit and talk awhile
I forgot just what it's like to purse my lips and smile

Runnin' C-Town

"I'm like a one-eyed cat, peepin' through a seafood store
Well I can look at you 'til you ain't a child no more."

Sweet, stickers of flesh rended outwards
If not to find a mate
Swimming to nip at habit's buds

Oh, but for your weight and texture
I lay with my mouth agape
Sweet stickers of flesh — rended outwards

Still of sunshine, still of wildfire
My appetite's still there — I already ate
Swimming to nip at habit's buds

O, but for the fruits of ire
I lay in wait to pollinate your eggs
Sweet stickers of ... flesh rended outwards

If the correct, only way was to be sure
Oh, but I love your very shape
Swimming to nip at habit's buds

And the feel of what's to come of eels
To set out upon yon river with a sail
Sweet stickers of flesh rended outwards
Swimming to nip at habit's buds

Hanging Garden Flower

Ah! he is not a common man
Who turns to a flowerless tree.
—Onitsura

Many leaves reside within her garden
Many leaves, indeed; many
Across the breeze the gray river
Golden Bridge, and lady's laughing faces
Many leaves, many slender: many
All possessed of a smothered envy

Sweet but for the flower ...
With its boisterous oranges, yellows, and indigos
The blossom standing neatly in the sun
Who would blame the keeper for a peak while on the run
A cricket lands gently upon his fishing line
Now, the blue moon watches soundly

Snow white-capped mountains shift restlessly behind
A glimpse will catch, most assuredly
The willows sing what the wind ordains
While the pond's low notes support in harmony
Her fringes sway askance within the wind
A late afternoon nap tucked between the folds

The blue plums taste so good this evening
The color of your eyes tantalize—I am mesmerized!
What if the moon saw your face?
Knowing distance wide your beautiful name

EUPHRATES ARNAUT MOSS

The swirling eddies only enhance the aura at once
And once again once I saw you again once
Apricot boughs and ferns seem as nothing

The now-cloudy skies are ever wanting
I could sit here and think and want the more
I that was once so dandy and sprightly
An American prince out of monarchy
Lie jealous of the folds and forays
Of my lady's Hanging Garden Flower

Prelude to Soil

Drunk off the waters of Lethe
I remember the harangues set against
A fugue which was transmitted
Through an ondes Martenot

I, having not known of the letter,
Planted 'neath the soil—your womb
In utero, my seed
A blackened child
Her new framed lullaby
Delivered to St. Peter
A weed of doubt stuck deep in my mind

Portraits de Ketchikan

1.
Behold, yonder! Take heed as nature clashes vehemently
with the land. 'Tis Alaska that lies beneath the will of the rain;
Alaska with its lands eternally wet.

O Alaska! with your lack of sophistication in a simple life!
O Alaska! with your incredible isolation from the world!

2.
Study the people and their habits of Fishin', Drinkin',
Huntin', and Lazin'.
Participate in their rituals of the Fourth,
And floating rubber ducks released into wild cascading rivers.
See the faux-city buildings all selling Jewelry to the Germanic
travelers, passing their way;
Watch the villagers communicate freely with each other as
they go about their lives —
All knowing All.

3.
Scan toward me;
Cast thine eyes yonder the emerald hills of dear Columbia —
Beyond, even, the ebon mining hills;
Look to the North and observe your man.

No different is he than the coal miner down in the mines,
Nor the police officer patrolling the tranquil town,
Nor the baker with his loaves of bread,
Nor the manager and all of her employees.

4.
O Alaska! Call to the East with your Western territorial voice.
Without you, I should surely not know of the wild,
Though I would think that I knew it.

Call forth with bears, who scavenge destitute motor vehicles,
And your minuscule airports stacked room-atop-room,
And your town which stands nearly as small,
And your highways, byways, triways, but no freeways.

5.
Frontier Alaska, separate from the rest of America,
Call to us, and remind us of ourselves.

Halo

I found this: a halo
For you, the other day;
The other day when I had stumbled
O so far as to mean to tell,
(Let's not sit and dwell)
To tell of how I felt for you
It's true but I would not dare to smack it
With my lips, adieu, a spank and then
Some colored licks for you, change tact
The way I speak is considered rude
I don't mean to have an attitude
But here we are again
Speaking of things that are true
But I don't want to say them
So I just criss-cross and backtrack
And ransack my mind for things
That came before this ill-fated ... turnaround
The man's insane and he don't love you
Not the way that I do
Hear you the playing of that accordion?
The ragged way it wheezes a distorted tune?
It's the way that other guy feels about you
And truly — truth be told, if I may be so bold
I am such a better man than him
And I can do better than to choke a hymn
With some keys that clearly stick
"The air is thick; but you are not
So why fool around this lot?" is what
I mean to say, but my tongue's stuck

EARLY HARVEST

So instead I tell you of the halo I found
And damn the ground, then and now
Somehow off the bow of a sinking ship
I might have bit off more than I can chew
I have little to nothing left to say to you
So I present you with this halo
And hope you'll understand just enough
It's rough, I know, but it'll do somehow
To show now, the right conditions
Not that I'm on a mission
To alienate ...

Soil

Clothes hanging
Down the lines and in rows
The clouds gently blotting out the sun
Move so slowly, methodically, asymmetrically
The pulley creaks; the clothes flip about like fish
The dampness of the clothes, love
I lie meditative, prone

A lark in the crack of noon
Tries yet to escape—(distant chimes)
The leaden weight unbilicus
Submerged in meconium fluid
Stabbing hanger hearts
(I'm so sorry)
I cannot bear yours any longer
My incised hand
Pain elicited blood red
A solipsis of the scalpel

Sun Wales moving apart
Still the cold steel—the churn
The slow-riding charm simply tossed off
(So casual)
Was there something more I desired?
Deep within the catacombs
Of a translucent cave
Dreams come up and make nest
Quicksilver girl, lime on the walls
They dissolve away the pain

EARLY HARVEST

(Did it hurt you, too)
Dusted up in the aftermath
Something more I never had
(Hush now, my darling. Dormes!)
Strange it is, our weakness
And yet you cannot do without us
Inhuman that you are
(I shall soon be far away)

For He doesn't suffer killers
(He burns them)
If this plan is to work
Then you mustn't take part
Who is he —
She that so clearly birthed us
(I can see the scars left behind)
Things must be done the right way
(Hell hath no fury)
What was conceived?
(Is it good for you?)
A dinner in your honor
(If I were with you tomorrow)
Would you still feel so far?
The madcap manic laughs
Belly rotunda
And salty seas of ...

Sun damaged skin
Perhaps in hiding

EUPHRATES ARNAUT MOSS

Where are you?
Bereft of a son
(And now for the main course)
Light the lamps, now burning
Slow motion commotion, like me
Yes, come love, kiss the flame
Sweet dandy like the bodies before
See the blue beginnings
Like the bluest of stars
That infinite "What If"
My candle, let me kiss you — my!
Incandescent — now snuffed

Silence

Many words passed
Commenced in each of two
They fell like so many pictures
As wine inside a glass
Until one had realized
Words were money in a purse

And so one took initiative
A gentle "hush" is what was said
The two just sat there quiet
Content until both died

PART II — Excess

God, No

God as conceived would have me vilified
To have his will turned to be tried, tested
That I could one day be beatified
So much lost for love, doubt to be denied
Eternal damnation for those who quested
For the truth out there that must be wrested
From those who seemingly have simply lied
But if I went into the underground
And my soul did not stop there but went on
Further beneath to the devil by the lake
I would ask how such a thing coud be sound
Punished to the last for thinking upon
The likelihood that God exists for sake

To Be Compared

To be compared is a most odious offense
Most especially when it is to that series of dread
Where numerous narrative flaws of sense,
Such ill-wrought passages, the much ado about the dead
Nothingness of a meaningless romance forced between
Two zero-dimensional characters—sometimes three
Interchangeable as the chessboard's pawns
Trying my patience for eternity.
You discuss love that need not speak its name
And make for a grandiloquent loquaciousness
In lieu of subjects bearing less than shame
Extending a hand of feigned sagaciousness
You deal worse than the rabbit in the briar
When you liken me to Stephanie Meyer

Arrangement

I would I'd lived in times of arrangement
Of the union of two; locked in marriage
With the dowry items in the carriage
Estranged from the concept of estrangement
Or accustomed in a way that suits me
Just so long as we could at least agree
Tied by an appropriate engagement
I don't understand the business of love
Granted, I have been in love times before,
A woman's love's a complicated score
A woman's feelings? Ask about the dove!
At one time it is there for me to hold
At another it is lifeless cold
And I wish with my all to be above

—27 April 2013

The Dantean Admission

There is a Dantean Admission
Ramified from The Divine Comedy
That more interesting people are in hell
Which explains Inferno's pre-eminence
Above the other epic's canticles
Like strains of secularity
Within the guise of a godly poem
A case of Virgil versus Beatrice,
Aquinas opposed to Aristotle;
Is Solomon wiser than Socrates?
But Greeks believed all suffered in after
Forever, regardless of good or bad;
And Romans took only purgatory.
So, what's to say of Christians and Atheists now?

— 1 December 2013

Grant Me a Woman

... Of what I could be
If Martha Bernays were my mother
And my mother is beautiful
And so (minding The psychoanalyst)
I greatly value beauty, of course

My mother is exuberant
Enough to swim a pool's length
Before she learned to swim
Lurching her way hunchbackingly
Desperate arms flailing; Slugger

God give me a Shakespearean woman
With wit and charm enough to boot
And a certain finesse to mingle;
Who appreciates the sweet life
And the boundless treasures it holds

Give me a woman of strength
And I mean strength of character, damnit!
Who won't roll over on me
But can still stick it to me
When I turn for the wrong

Give me a woman who inhales spirit
And sweats life for the life of me!
Grant me a woman of endless love
Who knows when to say what
When to accept what I have to give

Severed Connexion

So I'm here on the grid
And I wonder if I'll meet someone
Someone worth knowing, worth seeing, worthy
I can see someone distant on the horizon

"How now, Young Buck," she'd say. Right.
"I don't understand you. I appreciate you, but someday
You'll find someone who will treasure your quirkiness.
I won't read you because I hate poetry
And I can't be your penpal now or soon
That's just not what I am here for
But I enjoyed our <u>brief</u> conversation."

Maybe so but I didn't enjoy it
I feel disheartened and uncomfortable
And I like human beings less now

—8 August 2011

Wild Mantra Evening

I make verbal acrobatics concrete as schematics
Clutch your semi-automatic tonight
Snort horse with the Doors and Jim Morrison's corpse
Is a portis you'll be riding in flight

Your throat is smote every stroke till it's grote
Every note is a dissonant theme
Then nymphs in charge with pupils so large
Barge in with cookies and cream

The pulchritudinous ever multitudinous
Now you're being rude with us, please
Speak straight don't placate aggravate
Crazy eight it with a bottomless tease

Make cheer this year with a queer kinda sneer
Get your beer you're gonna need it now
Some huck butt fucked the car with a "shucks"
And got mucked with stuff from a cow

She was scalded by the pan
Sent back by attacks in from the deuce among the men
Scalded by the pan
She went down but never came up

Some harlequin harlot turned her face out real scarlot
Said, "Varlot, I've got swing and sass,"
I stepped into the spotlight not sure if I'm cockright
And spun my wheels with the gas

EUPHRATES ARNAUT MOSS

Where little Bopeep got it on with a creep
"What's wrong, soldier, ain't you doing fine?"
So I turned her loose like she's tied to a fuse
Said, "Sorry, I ain't your kind!"

Somnambulatory with a different kind of story
In the laboratory glory of me
Steel trap where that moose cap brain fapped
Gets slapped, is where I'd rather get free

Some shooter outside with a scooter on a slide
In the mood for suicide under glares
Has packed his junk in the left upper bunk
When he's feeling sorta sunk he just stares

The jack of all trades backed an ace on my spade
With a lady he laid so I caved
His head spooled dead with a tool from the shed
Made his bed and then I said, "Close shave."

That hit off the snowcone frost bit in the blowzone
Made me sit and then slow groan in bliss
That ship that has left slipstream real bereft
By a meaningful theft, it took the piss

She was scalded by the pan
Sent back by attacks in from the deuce among the men
Scalded by the pan
She went down but she never came up

Working Loathing: A Sestina

Fie on the day that I am made to work
For work is a place where people would clash
And it is so much harder with a boss
Who looks over your shoulder that you suffer
There is nothing you can do to flourish
But he finds fault in it; you must abide

And you say, "No! I will never abide
This pain in the ass that they call work,
Which drowns all the hope I have to flourish."
And so you and your peers must always clash
Making it even worse that you suffer
For they are the ones kissing up to the boss

And now you hate those who are like the boss
The idiots even less you can abide
For they even more will make you suffer
Because you get blamed for all their bad work
Forcing you and the boss to have to clash
Further damping your chances to flourish

You hope there is not a day he'd flourish
This evil man whom you must call a boss
How will you ever leave this place of clash
Which you are convinced no man can abide?
And now you dread the day you started work,
The cause of everything you must suffer

EUPHRATES ARNAUT MOSS

You really know what it means to suffer
The company scapegoat that can't flourish
The one they always choose to whip at work
Hated most of all by that awful boss
That man you know you cannot long abide.
There was never a time you didn't clash.

It stings and smarts, this awful bitter clash
No one else is this much made to suffer
Quitting is the thing you now can abide
You fantasize that you for once flourish
That you can sail far away from that boss
And never again will you have to work

The clash is ended; you can now flourish
You don't suffer now that you've quit the boss
But you abide that one day you must work

—11 April 2013

Breakfast All Day

The Argument

  I was part of a narrative poetry course when a fragment from an early version of "Breakfast All Day" (written for the class and available in its original incarnation at vox poetica) was shown on a transparency projection for the class to tear apart. All of the students were subjected to a blind criticism session in which their poetry would be evaluated uncredited. We were trying to determine whether the poem was worth reading—to find out whether it was compelling.

  "Now," said the instructor, "who wants to read the rest of the story?" Most of the class rather sheepishly raised their hands as their answer: the professor looked a bit bemused. "I mean is this a worthy poem? Is it worthy of poetry?"

  "Yes ... " one student answered, equally sheepishly.

  "But, I mean so many places serve breakfast all day." There was a note of impatience in her voice at this point.

  " ... Not McDonald's," mumbled another student.

  I got congratulations on the poem throughout the rest of the quarter when my peers asked me which poem I did (none of us ever took that anonymous thing seriously). But it's not just an example of an everyday victory of the proles uprising in union against the "owners of the means of production [read: knowledge]." It's also an example of the kind of snobbery we experience every day—snobbery that leads uneducated people to conclude that William Shakespeare's plays were composed by the better-educated, better-traveled, less intelligent, Edward De Vere. The same as the snobbery of the people who refuse to credit the writing of Rowling as literary or even good because everybody and their grandmother seems to love Harry Potter.

Who is to say what literature is? What poetry is? I don't have the answer, but I knew immediately that I was on the right track the day those events occurred. I was doing something right for the people. And it doesn't matter whether they like or dislike McDonald's or whether what I did was light verse. If it is light verse, by the way, I'd humbly hope it was so in the same way that Vince Guaraldi's music could've been called "light jazz."

The instructor actually asked me later on whether I wanted to be a composer of light verse. I was composing nothing but the stuff for the class because it was less time-consuming. What kind of question is that, though? Of course I want to compose light verse. What the hell do you think *The Importance of Being Earnest* is? Where on Earth would we be without Jeeves and Wooster? The truth is that I take it the same way as I take rhyme. A lot of people don't like it in this day and age but if it's good enough for Philip Larkin and TS Eliot, then it's certainly good enough for me.

The Poem

—Prologue—
Jimmy wanted breakfast for
The first meal of his day
"Son of a bitch!" he exclaimed
When the place told him it's not
Breakfast time, it's much too late
"It's 11:01 now."
"Where will I go for hotcakes?"

38

EARLY HARVEST

Exclaimed Jimmy in dismay,
"Breakfast burritos? Orange juice?
McMuffins, hash browns, coffee?
What ever will I do now?"

— Part1 —
When he went to upper brass
About his big decision
They rejected Jeb Marshall
But he went through anyway
And now he makes the big bucks
Because breakfast always works.
People got their sandwiches
Of egg or sausage all day
The pigs said "Hip hip hooray!"
Well, not everyone was glad
There was an evil person
Who gave Jeb Marshall a call
"Hello?" he answered the phone.
"Listen, sonny Jeb, to me,
I call the shots in this town."
"Right you are," said Jeb Marshall,
"But I want to know who's this?"
"Shut up! Now you listen here — "
Jeb could now tell who it was —
"This is what I have to say:
You're going to shut down now
None of this breakfast all day

We own this place, we're McWorld
McD's is your kind of place
But you have to know right now
It's my way or the highway.
You understand me, Marshall?"
"I understand you clearly,
R-R-R-Ronald," gulped Jeb.

—Part 2—
Now there was devastation
Within all this freedom land
For Jeb's McD's was shut down
And those nonbreakfast hours
Became a tribulation
A trial for us in the land
Because what were we to do?
"Have you had your break today?"
They would ask, but we haven't
We could no longer smile wide
Or even put a smile on
What you want is what you get
But we certainly didn't.
Did somebody say McD's?
Do you believe in magic?
How could McDonald's do this?
What's with McDonald's today?
It's not just food, folks, and fun
We certainly know better
McDonald's—It can happen

40

EARLY HARVEST

There's nothing quite like McD's:
"Good time, great taste (that's why this
Is our place)" truly sums it
"What can I possibly do?"
Asked Jeb Marshall that one day
Asked Jeb Marshall that one day
"The God McFather Donald
Is threatening our way of life
McDonald's and you, and us
That clown will not let us be."
Jimmy, Jeb Marshall's good friend
Placed hand on his chin in thought,
"Hmmm, I know what we can do."
And Jimmy formed up a crew
Of misfit rebel rangers
"It's gonna be Mac tonight!
Ron may have all the power,"
Jim said, "He may have the clout,
He will never take the one thing
That we cannot do without.
Re-open that McDonald's
And serve breakfast all day long
For we shall protect you
And in that, you can't go wrong."
Jeb clenched his fist, "God damn!
When you're right, you're fucking right.
Nobody makes your day like
McD's can, and we'll make theirs

You deserve a break today
And what better than our fast
To break for the entire day.
It's a good time for the great
Taste of McDonald's, alright!
Blessed are the hungry, Jim,
For they shall have their breakfast.
Even if it's at midnight!"
He re-opened McDonald's
With breakfast served all day long

—Part 3—
Ronald of the McDonald's
The clown of the family
The big boss of upper brass
Whose twisted smile told you that
He would best be reckoned with
Brought Jeb Marshall in one day.
"You know what this means, don't you?"
Jeb nodded his head, and said,
"I think I know exactly,
You and your goons are hard-set,
Y'all are gonna rough me up."
"Not just that," said Ron McD,
"We'll make you an example."
"Not if I have the first say!"
Then Jeb punched that clown real hard
And Ron went backwards falling,

EARLY HARVEST

"Wahahahahou!" he laughed
Bounced back with an uppercut
With clownish agility
Sent Jeb twenty feet flying
So Jeb was stuck in a cage
He's been brought to the circus
To be shown off to heads of
Corporate conglomerates
And yuppity uppity
Fatcats and bigwigs, warning
Nobody should toe the line.
But we did storm the ramparts
Put the bun on hamburglar
Made even Grimace grimace
Even the birdie would sing
But the clown was a tough one
He disoriented us
With balloons and other things
He sprayed us down with seltzer
Then he honked his horn aloud
And grabbed me around the neck
Oh, he had the upper hand
But I knew the clown's weakness
I brought out a small kitten
And to tell of what that cat
Did to poor Ronald would be
Above the powers of words.
And then Jimmy, who appeared,
Put old Ronald's hands behind

In handcuffs for safety's sake
"So," said Jeb, "what will you do?
Will you let us have breakfast?"
"Never!" cried the red-haired clown
But Jimmy had a good grip
And he hoisted up his arms
Causing poor Ronald to say,
"Augh, you son of a bitch, you.
Alright. you can have breakfast."

—Part 4—
So all the land had rejoiced
And the people lived in peace
"I think," said Jimmy, "we won."
"No," said Jeb, "everyone won."
But then Larry the Leopard
Jumped out from his hiding spot
"What the fuck?!" exclaimed Jimmy
"Nobody can do it like
McDonald's can," said Larry,
Looking threatening to the group
But Jeb knocked Larry out cold
With a hydrant to the head
'Cause sometimes things get stupid
Sometimes things just aren't alright
Advertising goes astray.
The best intentions go wrong
But it's McDonald's today

EARLY HARVEST

And well on in the future
No one could stand in the way
And with breakfast back in force
All the folks lived happily,
Happily ever after.

Euphrates Arnaut Moss has been writing since age 3 or so. He was born on October 18, 1985. He attended Bellevue Community College, where he was accepted for a contributing writer's position as part of the staff of the college newspaper despite having no experience or qualifications. He received a token half pay and considers those writings to be "illegitimate sketches." He went on to attend Portland State University for a short stint and Seattle University, graduating with a BA in English/creative writing. He considers his greatest influences to be James Joyce, Mark Twain, Emily Dickinson, and William Shakespeare.

Publication Credits

Special acknowledgment is made to the following publications for graciously publishing original versions of some of the poems appearing in this collection:

Amulet: "Prelude to Soil"
Eskimo Pie: "Prelude to Soil"
Languageandculture.net: "Soil"
Love's Chance: "Silence"
Mad Swirl: "Runnin' C-Town"
The Sheltered Poet: "Hanging Garden Flower," "Portraits de Ketchikan"
Soul Fountain: "Halo"
The Stray Branch: "Moth"
vox poetica: "Breakfast All Day"
The Write Place at The Write Time: "Severed Connexion"

Selected Titles Published by Unbound Content

www.ingramcontent.com/pod-product-compliance
Lightning Source LLC
Chambersburg PA
CBHW031154090426
42738CB00008B/1322